SUPERSTARS!™
ONE DIRECTION

SUPERSTARS!™
ONE DIRECTION

SUPERSTARS!™
ONE DIRECTION

PRODUCED BY

DOWNTOWN BOOKWORKS INC.

President Julie Merberg
Senior Vice President Patty Brown
Editorial Assistant Sara DiSalvo
Special Thanks Sarah Parvis, Caroline Bronston, Emily Simon, Melissa Rosenberg, and Laura Levin

Writer Sunny Blue
Design www.reitdesign.com/Our Hero Productions

Time
HOME ENTERTAINMENT

Publisher Richard Fraiman
Vice President, Business Development & Strategy Steven Sandonato
Executive Director, Marketing Services Carol Pittard
Executive Director, Retail & Special Sales Tom Mifsud
Executive Publishing Director Joy Butts
Editorial Director Stephen Koepp
Director, Bookazine Development & Marketing Laura Adam
Finance Director Glenn Buonocore
Associate Publishing Director Megan Pearlman
Assistant General Counsel Helen Wan
Assistant Director, Special Sales Ilene Schreider
Design & Prepress Manager Anne-Michelle Gallero
Brand Manager, Product Marketing Nina Fleishman
Associate Prepress Manager Alex Voznesenskiy
Associate Production Manager Kimberly Marshall

Special Thanks To Christine Austin, Jeremy Biloon, Stephanie Braga, Jim Childs, Susan Chodakiewicz, Rose Cirrincione, Lauren Hall Clark, Jacqueline Fitzgerald, Christine Font, Jenna Goldberg, Hillary Hirsch, Suzanne Janso, Mona Li, Amy Mangus, Robert Marasco, Amy Migliaccio, Nina Mistry, Dave Rozzelle, Adriana Tierno, Vanessa Wu, Elizabeth Bland, Robin Micheli

ISBN 10: 1-60320-950-6
ISBN 13: 978-1-60320-950-2

We welcome your comments and suggestions about Time Home Entertainment Books. Please write to us at:
Time Home Entertainment Books
Attention: Book Editors
P.O. Box 11016
Des Moines, IA 50336-1016

If you would like to order any of our hardcover Collector's Edition books, please call us at 1-800-327-6388, Monday through Friday, 7 a.m. to 8 p.m., or Saturday, 7 a.m. to 6 p.m., Central Time.

CONTENTS

One Direction Obsession 6

Sprint to Superstardom! 8

"Up All Night" With...Harry Styles.....................18

"What Makes You Beautiful" Niall Horan 24

Coming to America 30

ID Down Under 44

"Gotta Be You" Zayn Malik 62

"Everything About You" Liam Payne 68

"Stole My Heart" Louis Tomlinson 74

U R Invited to ID Concert Mania! 80

Heart-2-Heart 90

5-On-5 Fun-O-Rama 94

Brit Speak 98

I.D. on ID 102

Meet and Greet...112

Fantasia..116

Test Your ID IQ 118

Identify the ID Quote...120

ID True or False Quiz...122

Caught on Camera! 124

Photo Credits...128

ONE DIRECTION OBSESSION

East, west, north, south…right, left, or straight ahead, whichever way you go today, it leads right to ONE DIRECTION! The awesome, amazing, and adorable Harry, Niall, Louis, Liam, and Zayn—One Direction—took less than a year to conquer the world of pop music. They built a 21st-century base of millions of fans across the globe through TV, Facebook, and Twitter. Girls all over the world are taking a cue from their debut album and are up all night listening to their hit singles, "What Makes You Beautiful," "One Thing," "Gotta Be You," and "More Than This." And many of those fans are lining up for their *Up All Night* tour, which has dates scheduled through the end of 2012. If you miss out on that one, the boys have already announced their tour dates for 2013.

On the following pages, you will see the lads at work and at play, joking around together, and giving their all to their fans. You'll learn how they started out, how they got their lucky break, and exactly how they infiltrated America to capture the hearts of fans just like you! You'll find tons of fun facts and trivia tidbits about their favorite things and heart-2-heart secrets. And let's not forget all the incredibly GORGEOUS photos you'll find in these pages.

So ready, set, go—in One Direction! The boys are waiting for you!

SPRINT TO SUPERSTARDOM!

(Left to right) Zayn, Louis, Niall, Liam, and Harry chill backstage at their 2010 *The X Factor* competition.

A very long time ago the British invaded America. No, not back during the Revolution! It was in the early 1960s, when an army of boy bands from the U.K. stormed our shores with their harmonies and shaggy haircuts and mod clothes. Led by the Beatles, these boy bands were comprised almost entirely of *really* cute guys, and girls on this side of the Atlantic welcomed them with open arms!

Now there's a new British invasion, thanks to One Direction. (Well, technically, it's a British *and* Irish invasion, because Niall Horan is from the Republic of Ireland!) While a lot of boy bands on today's scene started out on shows on Nick and the Disney Channel, the five cute guys from One Direction were discovered in the U.K., and became the protégés of none other than Simon Cowell, the *American Idol* judge who left the show in 2010.

That's the same year the 1D guys—Harry Styles, Niall Horan, Louis Tomlinson, Zayn Malik, and Liam Payne—each competed individually as solo acts on Britain's *The X Factor*. While they didn't make the cut, they took guest judge Nicole Scherzinger's suggestion and formed a band—and this time they landed a spot! They didn't win the competition, but Cowell, creator of *The X Factor*, immediately signed them to his label.

Cowell knew they would be huge, he told *Rolling Stone*, from the moment they auditioned for the show—"when they came to my house in Spain and performed, after about a millionth of a second. I tried to keep a straight face for a bit of drama for the show. I remember sitting next to this girl who I was working with. The second they left I jumped out of my chair and said, 'These guys are incredible!' They just had it. They had confidence. They were fun. They worked out the arrangements themselves. They were like a gang of friends, and kind of fearless as well."

In September 2011, 1D's first single, "What Makes You Beautiful," debuted at No. 1 in the U.K. By March of the following year, their first album, *Up All Night*, debuted at No. 1 in the U.S. on the *Billboard 200* chart. No other British band ever saw their first album debut here at No. 1!

The British are definitely here—and we bet you're very glad they've arrived.

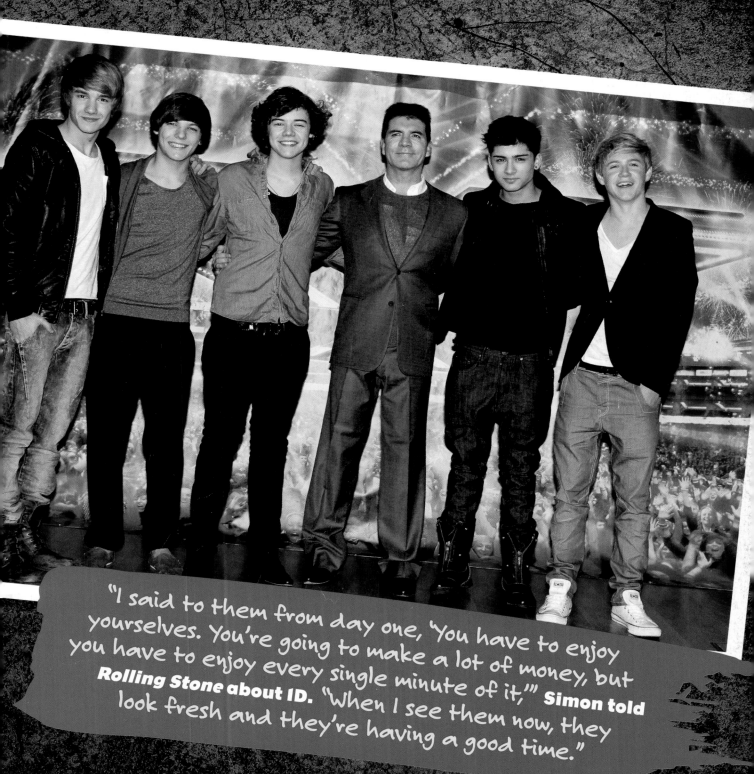

"I said to them from day one, 'You have to enjoy yourselves. You're going to make a lot of money, but you have to enjoy every single minute of it,'" **Simon told Rolling Stone about 1D.** "When I see them now, they look fresh and they're having a good time."

U.K. SINGLE LAUNCH ON SEPTEMBER 11, 2011
"What Makes You Beautiful"

"What Makes You Beautiful," first hit the airwaves and internet stream in Europe, New Zealand, and Australia on September 11, 2011. The release of their first single debuted at No. 1 on the British charts and it started One Direction infection all over. On that one day the guys made three launch appearances in Glasgow, Scotland, and Manchester and London, England.

The boys of 1D were jumping for joy the day their first single was released.

1D fans, known as the Directioneers, became a feverish flash mob the day "What Makes You Beautiful" was released!

2011 GQ AWARDS & 2012 BRIT AWARDS

Before the release of their single "What Makes You Beautiful" and their CD *Up All Night* in Britain the boys of 1D began showing up on red carpets across the U.K.

Sharp dressed: The boys look smart in skinny ties and black suits arriving at the U.K. *GQ* Men of the Year Awards in London, September 2011.

A Matched Set: The guys snagged Best British Single at the 2012 BRIT Awards in London, February 2012. Liam tweeted fans: "We have had such a great year and this is the start of a new one we owe so much to you guys can't thank you enough thank you 1DFamilyWW xxx"

ET CANADA & SNL

Next stop…North America. One Direction hit the shores of the former British colonies to greet super-excited fans, who chanted "We Love 1D!"

Face Off: The boys take tea on the set of *ET Canada* in March 2012.

1D received a coveted invite to guest on *Saturday Night Live*. They sang "What Makes You Beautiful" and "One Thing" on the April 7, 2012, broadcast and even hammed it up with the show's regulars in a skit called "The Manuel Ortiz Show."

"UP ALL NIGHT" WITH...

Born in Cheshire, England, Harry Styles has one thing in common with the Cheshire Cat in *Alice In Wonderland*—both always seem to be smiling! Known as the "Flirty One," Harry is also famous for his bouncy brown curls and cheeky personality. Let's see...Curls, smile, cheeky personality, big flirt—yep, they all add up to one pretty irresistible guy! The youngest of the five 1D idols, Harry began pursuing his dream of becoming a pop star at the age of 14, as the lead singer in a band called White Eskimo. That was just two years before he auditioned for *The X Factor*, which of course led to 1D and its stunning success.

Now Harry's a certified pop star, but one thing hasn't changed: he still tells bad jokes! "I always tell [the guys] jokes, then everyone goes silent," he told *Bop*. "They all shake their heads and say to me, 'That wasn't funny.'" It's okay, Harry. We love you just the way you are, bad jokes and all!

Says bandmate Louis: "Harry really does flirt with literally EVERY girl." (*Bop*)

"I like someone who likes a laugh!"
—Harry Styles (*Teen Now*)

HARRY STYLES

SPOTLIGHT ON HARRY

For his very first date... "I watched a film at my house with a girl. I don't remember what we watched though!" (*Seventeen*)

Before The X Factor... "I was just like every other teenager at school, and had a weekend job in a bakery.... I was in a band with some friends from school, and had watched *The X Factor* religiously when I was younger. It was a family thing to watch with my mum. We sat there [watching] the finale the year before we were on it and I said, 'I actually want to have a go at it one day.' Then my mum put the application in and came up to me just a few weeks later and [said], 'You've got an *X Factor* audition on Sunday,' and I was like 'What?!'"
(*102.7 KISS-FM On Air With Ryan Seacrest*)

He wouldn't want to go, um, head-to-head with Zayn in... "The strongest jaw line and pout competition." (*GL*)

How does Harry feel about screaming Directioneers?... "It's exciting and can get a bit overwhelming. I've been grabbed ... a couple of times, which was weird!" (*Teen Now*)

Harry's favorite late-night snack spot is... "This great Indian restaurant [near the London apartment he shared with Louis]—it's called the Royal Bengal. It is beautiful, so I do that...I go there loads and get myself a nice curry."
(*The People*)

"I think if you like someone, then it doesn't matter if they're a fan or not, but it would be a bonus if they liked the group!" —Harry Styles (Twist)

"We're so proud of the album. Honestly we just worked really hard making it."
—**Harry Styles (*Twist*)**

"WHAT MAKES YOU BEAUTIFUL"

The only non-English member of 1D is Niall Horan, who grew up in the small town of Mullingar, Ireland. Singing was his first love. "There are videos of me as a kid walking around singing and playing the guitar at maybe 4 or 5 years of age," Niall told *Life Story*. "I was always a big Frank Sinatra fan from a very young age; I don't know where I caught that. I might have just heard it on the radio. Maybe my family had some CDs, but I was always a singer and a mover."

Today Niall's musical tastes run to Justin Timberlake, Justin Bieber, Michael Bublé…and, of course, a little band known as One Direction!

And now, Niall is noticing that 1D is getting Bieber-fever level attention! He compared the first time they came to the U.S. when they were shooting "What Makes You Beautiful" in Malibu, CA, last summer, to when they returned to release *Up All Night* in 2012: "When we were here the last few times, we had maybe 20 or 30 girls at the airport and at our hotel and stuff," he told *Life Story*. "This time when we arrived at LAX there were 500 girls—the power of YouTube and Twitter is just proving itself in how teenagers pick up on things so quickly. We couldn't believe what we were seeing, the whole scene outside the hotel all week!"

And that was before they hit the road for the *Up All Night* tour.

Who knows how many girls would stay "up all night" to get a glimpse of 1D!

> "I like someone who can take a bit of banter!"
> —**Niall Horan**
> (*Teen Now*)

NIALL HORAN

SPOTLIGHT ON NIALL

Really? Me?... "Every now and then you have a realization moment where you get goose bumps and think, 'I am literally the luckiest person in the world.' It happened [when]…we played Dublin…I was standing in the biggest arena in the country, in front of 12,000 people, and they were screaming my name, and it's just like, 'What is going on here?'" (*onedirectionfans.net*)

Kitchen whiz... "I cook a lot. I did a spaghetti Bolognese one day, did fajitas another and then beans and cheese on toast. The last one sounds lazy, but you cannot underestimate it—it's easy and tastes delicious." (*The People*)

Punch drunk... "In the evenings, the giddiness kicks in. It's kind of like we go mad. We were sitting in the studio yesterday all trying to make each other laugh, and Zayn was making faces behind the producer's back. It was just pure childishness!" (*Top of the Pops*)

A toast To Niall... When 1D visited the Australian morning show, *Sunrise*, Niall tried the national breakfast staple—toast and Vegemite spread. Polite, but not eager to finish it, Niall ate only half. The other half didn't go to waste—the show host auctioned the half slice of toast for the Australian charity YoungCare —it went for nearly $100,000! Yummy!

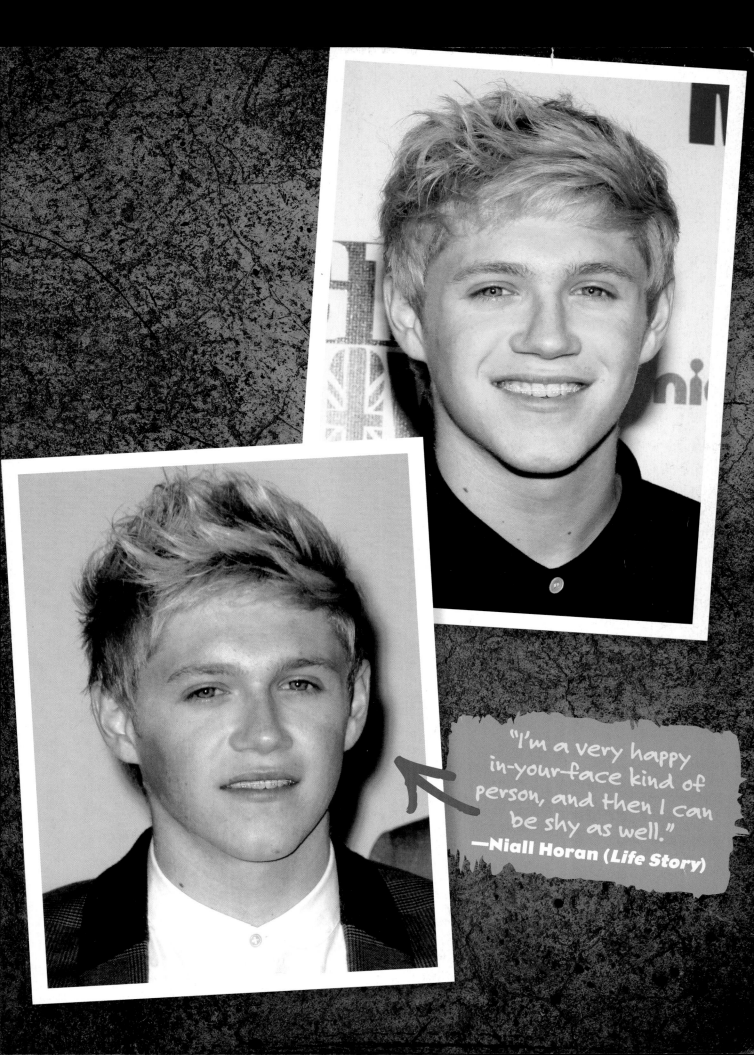

"I'm a very happy
in-your-face kind of
person, and then I can
be shy as well."
—Niall Horan (Life Story)

(Left to right) Zayn, Louis, Liam, Niall, and Harry sang their hearts out to support the BBC's Children in Need event, November 2011.

COMING TO AMERICA

When 1D first arrived on these shores, only their most dedicated U.S. fans were paying attention. Already a sensation in the U.K. after their third-place showing on *The X Factor* but not widely known here, the five lads traveled to California in August of 2011 to film the video for "What Makes You Beautiful" on the beaches of Malibu.

In November, though, One Direction stepped boldly out of stealth mode and launched a full-out assault on the U.S.: The band announced it would open for Big Time Rush on several dates of its U.S. tour beginning in February 2012. By late January, when the boys flew "across the pond" again to tape an episode of *iCarly* in Los Angeles, "What Makes You Beautiful" was well on its way to racking up 50 million views on YouTube— a milestone it hit on Feb. 8—and the boys were met with widespread fandemonium across the country.

The battle was over almost before it began. Hordes of American girls had already surrendered and signed up as full-fledged Directioneers!

"We're going to go out and give it our best shot. We really just want to go out and see what happens."
—Liam on 1D's hopes of breaking out in America, *J-14*

It was supposed to be a secret mission, but when 1D arrived at the Los Angeles International Airport in January 2012 to tape a guest appearance on an iCarly episode, the word was out—500 fans waited hours to catch a glimpse of their idols! But U.S. marshals on the flight decided it wasn't safe for the boys to disembark to greet the crowd. Harry tweeted: "Sorry that we couldn't stop at LAX

Niall, Harry, Liam, and Louis chill before a concert at the Patriot Center in Fairfax, VA, in March, 2012. Zayn was missing because he'd returned to the U.K. for a few days after learning that a family member had passed away.

1D + BTR=OMG!

1D came out to congratulate their tour mates Big Time Rush at the March 2012, premiere of *Big Time Movie*. (Left to right): Liam Payne, Logan Henderson, Louis Tomlinson, James Maslow, Harry Styles, Carlos Pena Jr., Zayn Malik, Kendall Schmidt, Niall Horan.

Niall, Liam, Zayn, Harry, and Louis got a standing O when they opened for Big Time Rush at New York City's Radio City Music Hall the following night. The audience sang along with them and chanted "We Love 1D!"

TODAY

When One Direction performed on the *Today show* in March 2012, avid Directioneers crowded Rockefeller Center hoping for a peek of—or a peck from!—the 1D sigh guys.

"Oh my God, I just loved them so much," a flustered fan from Philadelphia told hollywoodlife.com. "We got up at one o'clock in the morning and we drove down here. We've been here since about four o'clock."

Asked to pick her fave 1D song, she just couldn't do it: "I like all their songs; I couldn't really choose.... I could listen to any of them and it makes me feel so happy."

The boys arrived via a double-decker tour bus and sang "What Makes You Beautiful," but they could hardly be heard above the excited crowd of fans. It didn't really matter—everyone seemed to know the lyrics and sang along with Harry, Niall, Zayn, Louis, and Liam!

ZAYN MALIK

HARRY STYLES

"For me, since we got put together, we made four best friends," **Zayn said on** *Today.* "For us, that's the most amazing part."

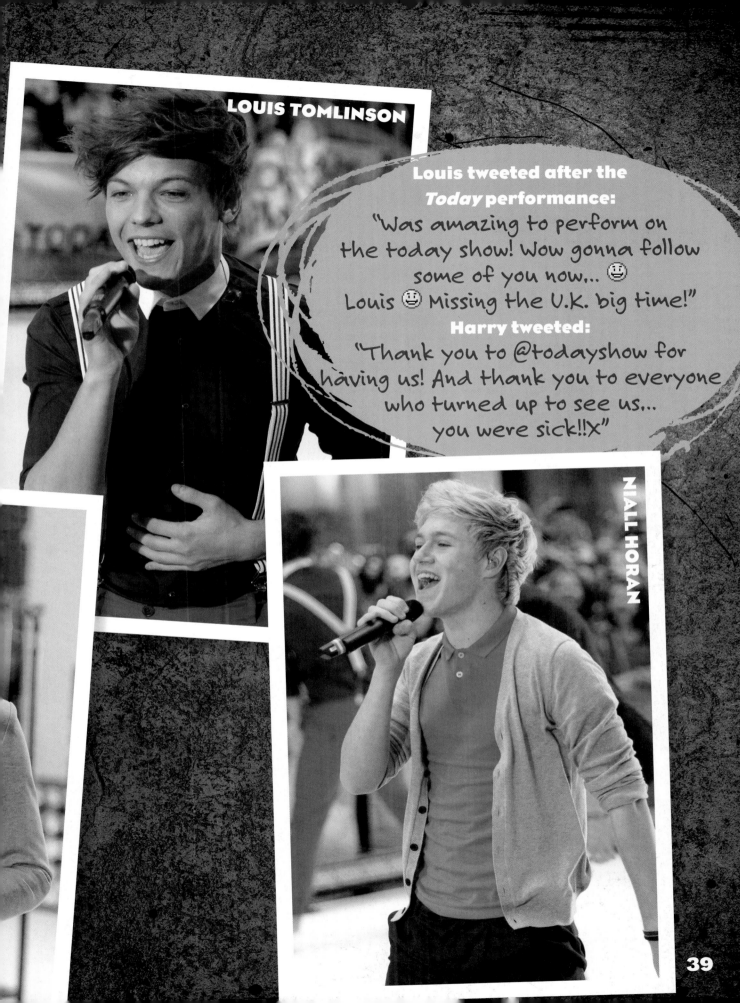

LOUIS TOMLINSON

NIALL HORAN

Louis tweeted after the *Today* performance:
"Was amazing to perform on the today show! Wow gonna follow some of you now... ☺
Louis ☺ Missing the U.K. big time!"

Harry tweeted:
"Thank you to @todayshow for having us! And thank you to everyone who turned up to see us... you were sick!!X"

39

AND THE WINNER IS...

More than 9,000 fans were on hand in the Dallas suburb of Frisco, TX, to welcome 1D to Dr. Pepper Ballpark in late March 2012, after Dallas won the online "Bring 1D to the U.S." contest. (The contest entailed a series of weekly challenges online; the city with the most participation won a special visit from the group.) The boys sang "Up All Night," "More Than This," "One Thing" and "What Makes You Beautiful"; did a question-and-answer session from the middle of the ball field, and signed autographs. According to the *Dallas Morning News*, some of the questions fans asked were, "Would you live in the United States?" "What most important person would you perform for?" and "How long does it take you to do your hair?" What would you have asked?

They came, they saw, they conquered: Eight thousand screaming fans showed up at the Mall of America in Bloomington, MN, to welcome 1D's British invasion. The boys signed 1,000 autographs! Can you say writer's cramp?

1D (hearts) NICK

1D wrapped up a triumphant month stateside by appearing at the Nickelodeon Kids' Choice Awards on March 31, 2012 (here with Kelly Osbourne). The boys were introduced to First Lady Michelle Obama and her daughters Malia and Sasha at the ceremony. Mrs. Obama invited them to the Easter Egg Roll at the White House but they had to decline because they were scheduled to be in Australia that day.

The *iCarly* episode 1D taped in January 2012 aired on April 7. Originally titled "iGot Jungle Worms," the episode was renamed "iGo One Direction." Hmm...much more appealing, don't you think!? On the show, Carly comes home sick from a trip and learns that 1D has agreed to perform "What Makes You Beautiful" on her Web series. Harry then gets sick after drinking from Carly's water bottle but it turns out he's faking it—he just wants Carly to nurse him back to "health!"
Catch it in reruns.

ID DOWN UNDER

1D DOWN UNDER

In early April 2012 Harry, Niall, Louis, Zayn, and Liam were off to Oz—or Australia, as it's also known! One Direction fan sites Down Under began the countdown for the band's arrival a week in advance, the anticipation heightening by the day, even the hour! They boys kicked off their stay on the continent with a visit to Sydney and an appearance on the Australian *Today* show, answering questions from fans in the audience. Next up: a whirlwind of personal appearances, radio interviews, and concerts in Sydney (two), Melbourne and Brisbane. But boys will be boys—the guys couldn't have an all-work-no-play trip, could they? No way. The five hotties took time to enjoy the beautiful sun and scenery of Sydney Harbour. Not satisfied with boating, fishing, and swimming, Liam and Louis then headed off to surf the waves of Sydney's Manly Beach. Now that's fun in the sun!

The guys laugh it up on Australia's *Today* show.

In the booth! 1D poses for a snap with DJ Jackie O from Australian radio's *Kyle* and *Jackie O Show*.

ONE DIRECTION!

Anchors away!

When One Direction first hit the shores of Sydney, Australia, in April 2012, they took time out for a little R&R. They headed right for a luxury yacht in Sydney Harbour and, of course, were dressed in proper boating attire for a day on the water—bathing suits, of course! They spent the day swimming, sunning, zipping around in a light craft, fishing, and just plain horsing around with each other. We're pretty sure at least one person got pushed into the water!

The day seemed to be just what Harry, Niall, Liam, Zayn, and Louis ordered. "Chilling big time today, Liam Payne went fishing and caught the boat," Niall tweeted to the band's Twitter followers. "What a great day! Really nice to chill with the lads!"

Zayn, Louis, and Harry take a spin around Sydney Harbour in a high-tech rubber dinghy!

What's caught Harry's attention? A playful porpoise? No, it's paparazzi with long-lens cameras!

Louis tries his hand with a rod and reel.

Louis encourages Liam. Niall would rather watch!

Come on, Harry! Do you really want us to believe that the fish that got away was *that* big?!!!

Uh-oh, did Liam catch a big fish? From the looks of his smile, it could be a mermaid!

AGS020N

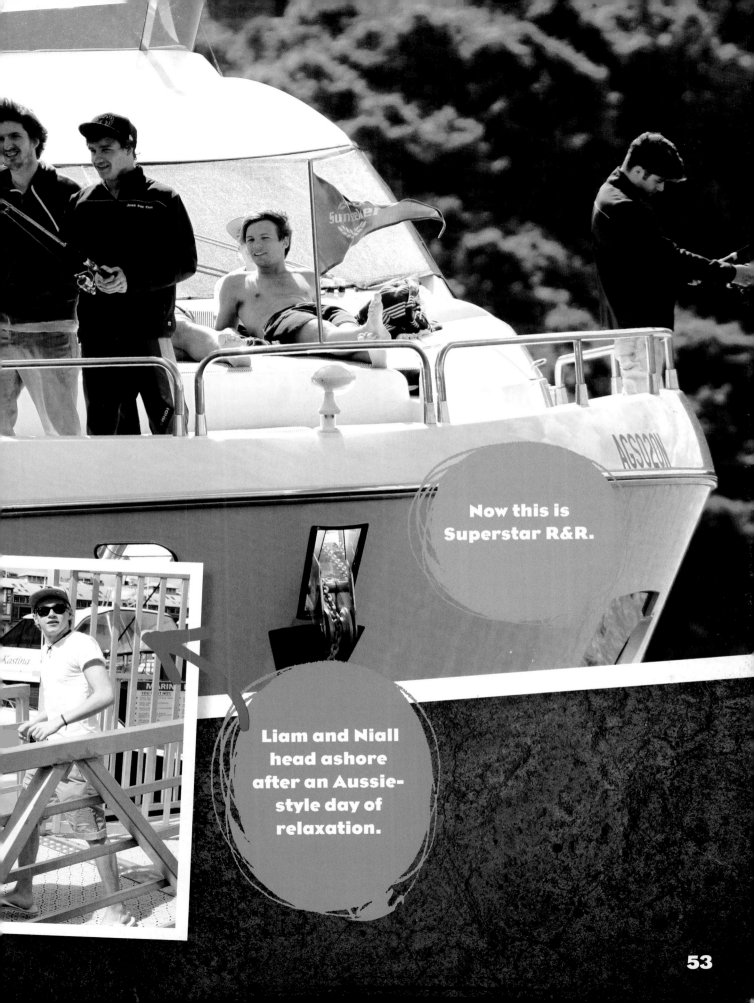

Now this is Superstar R&R.

Liam and Niall head ashore after an Aussie-style day of relaxation.

LIAM & LOUIS HEAD IN ONE DIRECTION— THE AUSTRALIAN SURF!

Hang Ten! Liam and Louis brought their surfboards to Sydney's Manly Beach and took a few practice moves on the beach before heading into the water. These two dudes were totally stoked at the thought of catchin' waves. Liam tweeted, "me and louis just went surfing…louis was up first and for a long 1 like 30 FEET!!!!!! OMG then I stood up on two nice waves woohoo :)"

1D GETS A KOALA CUDDLE!

During 1D's April visit to Oz, they wanted to sample everything truly Australian. Nothing is more "Down Under" than a koala, so Harry, Niall, Louis, Zayn, and Liam visited the Lone Pine Koala Sanctuary in Brisbane. Before meeting the super-cute critters, the guys learned some interesting facts. Australians never refer to koalas as "koala bears" because they aren't bears! They're marsupials, like kangaroos, and their only natural habitats are in Australia. They were dubbed "bears" by English settlers who arrived in Australia in the 1770s and thought the little animals looked like bears.

After the biology lesson, 1D got up close with Kat the Koala, who curled up in their arms right away. (After all, wouldn't you?) She must be a 1D fan—she didn't want to leave Harry's arms! 1D know a good photo op when they're in one—they tweeted pictures of themselves and their "host," Kat the Koala.

Fun Fact: koalas like all marsupials, carry their babies in pouches.

HHH! 1D SURPRISES AUSTRALIA'S TV FANS

ne Direction's visit to Australia sparked rumors that the group would show up at the Logie Awards, Australia's equivalent of the Emmys, which were set for April 15. After all—the guys were right there in the country doing their promotional tour! But up until airtime, there had been no announcement that they would attend the ceremonies. As the attendees gathered in Melbourne's Crown Casino after walking the red carpet, there was no sign of Harry, Louis, Niall, Zayn, or Liam. Everyone was seated and prepared for a night of cheering on the winners of Australia's top TV award, the Gold Logie, when the opening bars of "What Makes You Beautiful" could be heard. The curtain was drawn and...ta-da! One Direction! They came on stage singing their hit song and looking adorable. What a way to start the night!

ONE! TWO! THREE! JUMP!

You can't go to Australia and not stop off in New Zealand, and that's just what One Direction did while they were Down Under.

They did the regular round of appearances, performances, autograph signings and radio visits. On a stop-by at New Zealand's 3 News, the boys talked about everything 1D, including a possible bungee jumping jaunt. Though they all agreed the extreme sport's name is hard to pronounce—Zayn tried, saying "BUN-gin joom-pin"—Louis and Liam decided to actually try their hand at it. So, Louis, Liam, and Harry went to Auckland's Sky Tower bungee jump to see what it was all about. Harry decided it wasn't for him and spent most of the time hanging out with the band's stylist and her baby daughter Lux. Meanwhile, Liam and Louis pulled on bright blue and yellow jumpsuits and strapped on the bungee harnesses. Woosh! They both jumped the 328-meter tower and bounced right back much to the joy of their crew and fans who there watching. Brave boys!

WEEEEEEE! Louis & Liam took their daring leap at Auckland's Sky Tower— fans were cheering them on ...and praying!

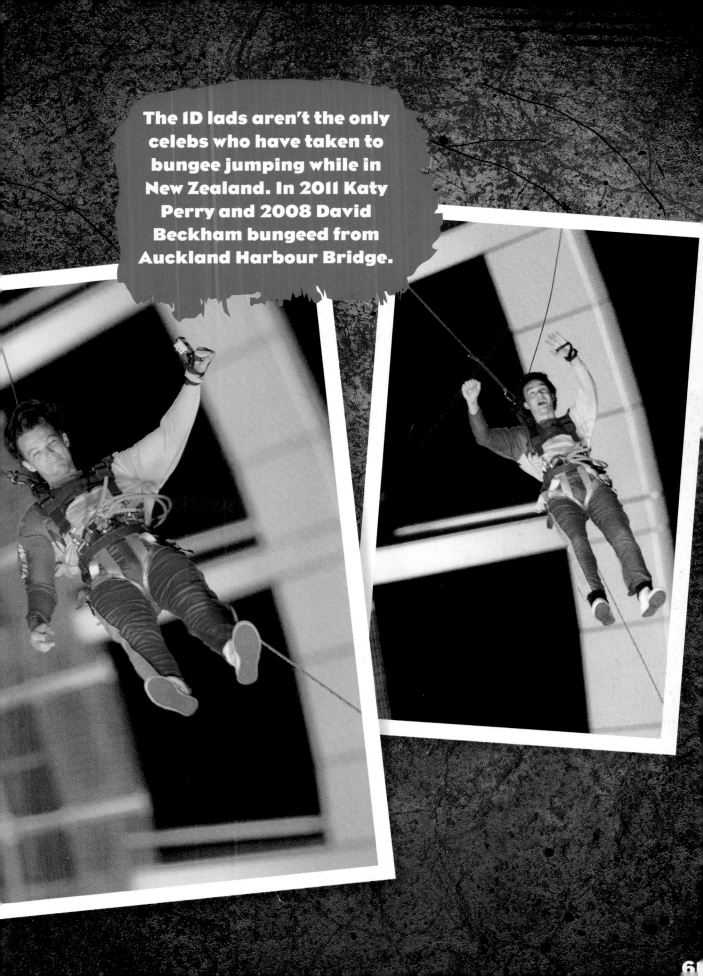

The 1D lads aren't the only celebs who have taken to bungee jumping while in New Zealand. In 2011 Katy Perry and 2008 David Beckham bungeed from Auckland Harbour Bridge.

"GOTTA BE YOU"

Zayn, whose father is of Pakistani descent, had the attention of three sisters, Doniya, Waliyha, and Safaa, when he was growing up in East Bowling, England, so it's no wonder that the totally crush-worthy guy we know today was always a bit of a peacock! "I was about 12 or 13 when I started taking pride in my appearance," he told *The Sun*. "I even used to get up half an hour earlier than my sister so I could do my hair. I had a few dodgy haircuts over the years. I shaved my head a few times and also had slits in my eyebrows. I thought I was properly gangsta, being into R&B and rap, and that it made me look hard."

Well, gone are the eyebrow slits and shaved head, but Zayn still takes pride in his appearance—and in his talent and success. He loves being in front of an adoring audience. "The noisier and bigger the crowd, the bigger the performance," he told *Life Story*. "You kind of always bounce off the crowd; you need a crowd!"

"I am a big believer in work hard, play hard!"
—**Zayn Malik**
(*Tatler*)

SPOTLIGHT ON ZAYN

Going in all directions... "I was a bit of handful when I was a kid because I was quite hyperactive. If I got the tiniest bit of sugar in me, I'd be bouncing off the walls." (*Life Story*)

"[Even as a baby] my mum used to put me in my pram because I was so full-on." (*The Sun*)

Flick fave... "*Scarface*—I love that film and Al Pacino."

Directioneer frenzy in the U.S... "Until we got to America, we didn't realize how crazy it was!" (*The Sun*)

Making "Beautiful" music together... "The minute we did ["What Makes You Beautiful"] we were like, 'This is our thing. This is our song. This is our sound,'" he told Ryan Seacrest. "We knew straight away, because it was completely different to anything we've heard before...we were like, 'This is the direction,' excuse my pun!"

1D pranks... "Harry shaved his initials into my leg hair. So I had a massive H. S., which wasn't too attractive!" (*Twist*)

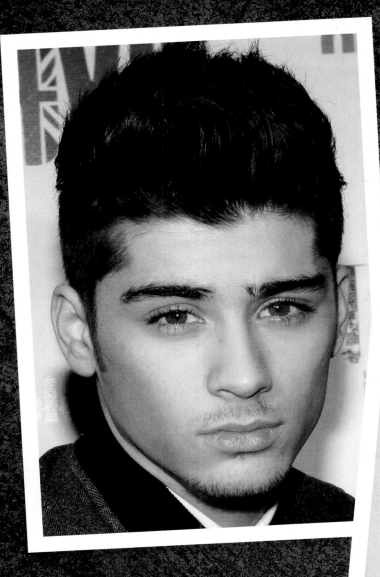

"...American girls are a lot more confident. They just come straight out and say what they have to say to you. The British girls are more shy, a little more reserved. American girls are straight to the point."
—Zayn Malik (*Life Story*)

How lucky can you get? Liam, Lewis, Niall, Zayn, and Harry at a CD signing on St. Patrick's Day 2012.

"EVERYTHING ABOUT YOU"

Born in Wolverhampton, England, Liam Payne got his first experience singing...in front of karaoke crowds! The young Brit quickly earned a local reputation for his voice and his dad encouraged him to enter singing competitions. "My dad used to watch *Pop Idol*, which was Simon Cowell's first show here in England," Liam told *Life Story*. [He] said, 'You should have a go at it.' When I was 14, I went on the show.... Got to the last 24 and got thrown out from there, and I figured I'd have another go in a few years, which eventually led to *X Factor*."

> "It's been amazing being over here in the States. We couldn't believe the [number] of people that showed up to the Today show.... We couldn't have asked for any more and we never really imagined any of this!" —**Liam Payne** (***On Air With Ryan Seacrest***)

Of course, *The X Factor* was Liam's huge break, but he never expected to find his future in harmony with four other singers. And he's been totally shocked by the fame they've encountered! "It's all happening so fast," Liam recently told *The Mirror*. "It's hard to take it all in."

But it's also fun, especially in the U.S., where, he explained to HitFix.com, the fans "will go to a lot further lengths to get noticed...The thing that really sticks out for me is a young lad [who] made a hat...out of Crayola markers and cello tape."

The lad with the hat may have been noticed, but One Direction can't go anywhere without *not* being noticed. And they seem to be having the time of their lives!

LIAM
PAYNE

SPOTLIGHT ON LIAM

Dressing room drama... "Louis takes the longest to get ready. It's all about his hair!" (*GL*)

Goofs and gaffes onstage... "Louis went on as a carrot! And another night, we were crouched down and Harry pushed me, and my trousers split—it was a massive rip!" (*J-14*)

Bad rap... "I think the whole thing, boy band, it's a little bit of a dirty word. They say it's not a good thing to be in a boy band. We want to change that. We want to make the boy band cool. It's not just about dancing and dressing the same." (*HitfFx.com*)

Terror tyke... "I was a bit of a naughty boy at school. I was often called into the headmistress's office...I used to have water fights in the toilets and climb on the roof to get footballs back!" (*The Sun*)

Oops!... "I walk into things. I'm a bit dopey. But Niall and Harry have both fallen over during a performance. Harry's is on YouTube!" (*GL*)

"I think we'd like to do more writing on the next album, but when you've got so many good songs coming at you, you can't turn down a good song."
—Liam Payne (*HitFix.com*)

"[Simon Cowell] has the final say on everything we do, so he is a huge, huge influence, but he gives us a lot of freedom at the same time. When we were doing the album, he allowed us to write with lots of different people."

—Liam Payne
(The People)

"STOLE MY HEART"

Born on Christmas Eve in South Yorkshire, England, Louis Tomlinson was indeed quite a gift—to his family and eventually to Directioneers everywhere! Even as a little boy, Louis was a natural at singing, acting, and making people laugh. A drama teacher encouraged him to try out for a part in a school production of *Grease* and he was cast in the lead role of Danny Zuko. From that point on, Louis knew music had to be a part of his life. He joined a band called The Rogue and in 2010 auditioned as a solo artist for *The X Factor*.

"Louis makes all of us lads laugh all the time. He is just the life and soul of the party."
—**Zayn Malik (*Bop*)**

In spite of Louis's—and the other 1Ders'—initial setbacks in the competition, success came pretty quickly for the guys, all teenagers when signed by Simon Cowell. But the guys were ready, says Louis. "We're young, but we've been forced to group up and we all have our heads screwed on right," he told *Life Story*. "If one person steps out of line, the other four will come down on him like a ton of bricks. We're really supportive of each other, but we've all agreed that if any of us do something that's not cool, the others will draw attention to it. That's one way to stay strong as a unit."

LOUIS TOMLINSON

SPOTLIGHT ON LOUIS

Why do his four little sisters need so many autographed posters?!...
"I think they must auction them off on the school bus!" (*Tatler*)

Date-night dress for success... "I hate wearing the same as everyone else, so I'd probably wear purple chinos—they sound disgusting but they look cool— and a polo or T-shirt and a cardigan. I love clothes, so I'd make sure I look nice." (*Teen Now*)

Wacko for Jacko... "I am a big Michael Jackson fan. He was a real inspiration and had so many great songs.... I'd like to adopt a chimpanzee and build an eternal friendship. That would be amazing." (*On Air With Ryan Seacrest*)

Burgers and Buns... "[One of the most] recent was when Niall was queuing for a Burger King or a McDonald's, and I just thought it would be funny to quickly pull his trousers down, and everyone saw. ... he still had his pants [underwear]. It was just his trousers." (*scholastic.com*)

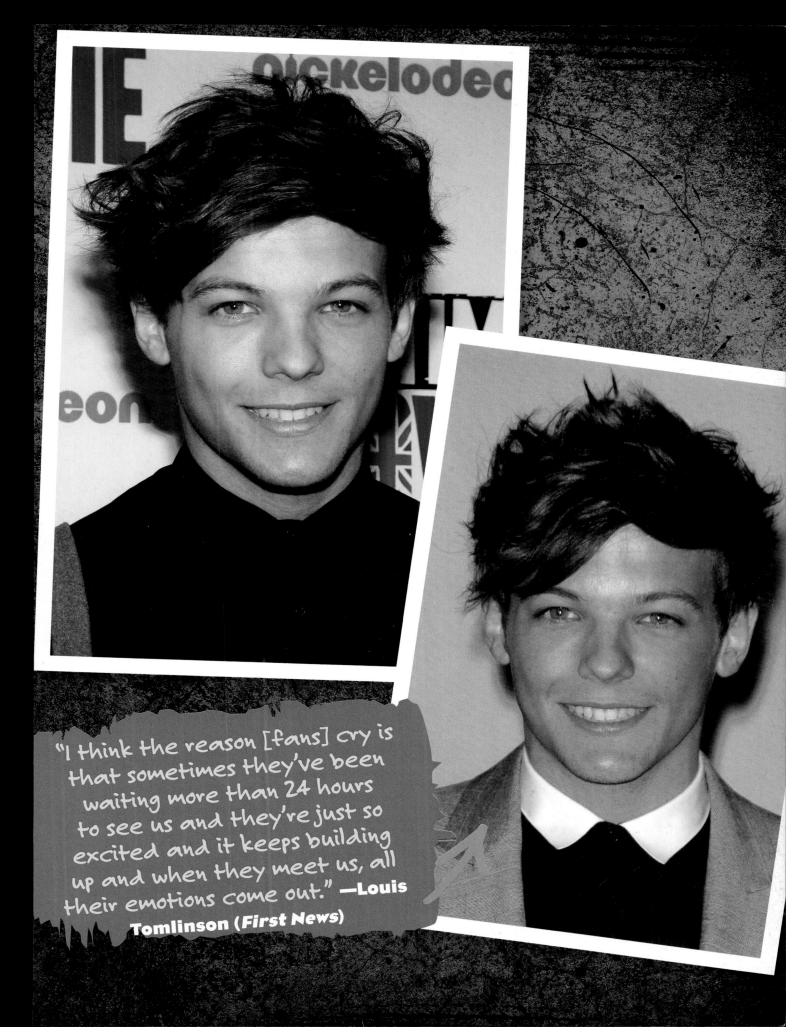

"I think the reason [fans] cry is that sometimes they've been waiting more than 24 hours to see us and they're just so excited and it keeps building up and when they meet us, all their emotions come out." —Louis Tomlinson (First News)

"... We keep each other grounded. We've got a great team around us helping us with that. We don't take ourselves too seriously, which I think is a big part of it as well. We know this is an amazing opportunity and we're just having fun with it, enjoying ourselves."

—**Harry Styles** (*Life Story*)

U R INVITED TO 1D CONCERT MANIA!

Do you have your One Direction concert tickets? Do you have your "I Love 1D" signs—or your face fan masks of Harry or Niall or Louis or Zayn or Liam? Do you know the lyrics to every one of the songs on *Up All Night*? Have you exercised your vocal chords in preparation for singing their songs and screaming their names? Are you ready to spend hours on line waiting to get into the venue? Are you prepared for fainting scenes and mega-decibel sound waves from screaming fans?

Well, if you have said YES to all of the above, you are a die-hard Directioneer—and we salute you! If you said no, that's okay, too! You can definitely be a true-blue Directioneer even if you can't get to one of their concerts.

The boys are spending a lot of time on the road these days. Their summer 2012 tour was set to kick off May 24 in Virginia then criss-cross the U.S. and Canada, and the guys are planning a December 3, 2012 appearance at New York City's Madison Square Garden, too. And in 2013, they take their act to their own stomping grounds with concerts in Great Britain and Ireland. Then they'll hop back to the U.S. and Canada. Whew! Harry, Niall, Louis, Liam and Zayn are going to be busy!

Whether or not you get to see them perform in person, check out some of 1D's tour stops en route to world domination!

ID lights up the night in Sydney Australia, April 2012.

In an interview with *MTV News*, Niall thanked Directioneers for their support: "The power of our fans, they never seem to stop amazing us. They're absolutely brilliant!"

ID guested on Saturday Night Live in April 2012. When the band found out about their booking, Niall told MTV News, *"Saturday Night Live is a big, big deal; everyone knows that! When we got invited, we couldn't believe it!"*

1D performed "Up All Night" and "What Makes You Beautiful" on the February airing of the British TV show *Dancing On Ice*.

Liam told *Seventeen* how 1D connects with their audiences:

"There's something we do at every concert where we get the crowd to sing with us. So far every crowd has sung along. It's so amazing to hear a crowd of people singing one of your songs. It's the best feeling!"

The boys performed on VEVO, the music video site, in April 2012

HEART -2- HEART

Flirt alert!... The guys of One Direction have won the hearts of girls across the world, but what wins *their* hearts? Harry, Niall, Louis, Zayn, and Liam are all very cute, but each boy has something special all his own. We bet you can pick one 1D boy that really makes your temperature rise! And just like you, each guy is attracted to a certain individual something in girls. Want to know what makes the lads stop, take notice, and stick around? Read on!

Boys Can Be Fickle Alert: This list may change at any time—they are boys, after all!

ZAYN:
Rosie Huntington-Whiteley
(British model/actress who appeared in *Transformers: Dark of the Moon*)

LOUIS:
Natalie Portman
(who starred in *Thor*)

LIAM:
Leona Lewis (British singer/
songwriter, who recorded the
best-selling single of 2008
worldwide, "Bleeding Love")

HARRY:
Kate Beckinsale (British
actress of the
Underworld series)

NIALL:
Demi Lovato of
Disney fame

GIRLS! GIRLS! GIRLS! ON THEIR MINDS

The 1D guys are just like any other guys when it comes to obsessing about the opposite sex. See what they are thinking …

Harry on Date Conversation:

"I went to dinner with a girl, and she just didn't speak! I started asking quite elaborate questions and I'm pretty sure she found some way to answer with a yes or no. It made me really tired. By the end of the night I was like, 'Thank God that's over!'"

(M magazine)

Liam on Heartbreak:

"I had a few dating disasters along the way with girls cheating on me. One girl was the inspiration for my singing 'Cry Me a River' on The X Factor. That was my payback to her because she was unfaithful."

(The Sun)

Zayn on the Girl of His Dreams:

"If [a girl is] intelligent and knows how to have a conversation, then I am won over. Nothing better than … sitting on the sofa and having a really nice, long chat. I sound all cheesy but I'm not really."

(The People)

Louis on his Very First Date:

"I went to the cinema on my first date. And the day before I was supposed to go, my date's friend came up to me and said, 'Are you going to pay for her?' And I was like, 'Why should I?' And she was like, 'That's what you're meant to do.' I was lucky she gave me a heads up!"
(M magazine)

Niall on the Perfect Date:

"A bit of dinner and a movie. You can't beat that. I like it to be chilled out. Or then you have the total opposite and go to a theme park and see how that goes, see how much fun she is. All regular teenage stuff."
(Life Story)

KISSY KISSY

Would the lads give a girl a kiss goodnight at the end of a date? They told *Teen Now*:

Louis: "Yeah, definitely, to show that I'm still interested."

Niall: "Yeah, but I'd just give her a peck on the cheek—keep 'em keen."

Harry: "Possibly. Actually, who am I kidding? If I liked her, then, yeah!"

Zayn: "Definitely!"

Liam: "I was hoping there would be one at the start of the night or in the cinema—that's why I [choose] the back row of the cinema!"

5-ON-5 FUN-ORAMA

Check out 1D's opinions on everything from the U.S. of A. to spaghetti Bolognese!

TOTALLY ALTERNATE-UNIVERSE JOBS

If the lads couldn't sing, what would they want to be?
(Teen Vogue)

Harry:
"An astronaut."

Zayn:
"A SWAT team member."

Liam:
"A fireman."

Niall:
"A soccer player."

Louis:
"A Power Ranger."

1D ON AMERICA

Harry's amazed by how friendly people are here... "Even people in the street. ... [they always ask], 'Hey, how you doing?'" (scholastic.com)

Zayn was amazed by the number of ID fans in the U.S.... "[Before we got here] we thought it could be the same few hundred people tweeting us over and over again,..." (*The Sun*)

Liam craves the food... "I came to America quite a bit as a kid. Applebee's is the best restaurant!" (*Twist*)

Louis loves the Big Apple... "Ever since I watched *Home Alone 2* as a kid, I knew I've wanted to go to New York City." (*Twist*)

Niall digs the West Coast vibe... "We love the USA, especially L.A. It's so relaxed and chilled out." (*Twist*)

1D REVEALS THEIR FAVORITE SONGS AND ARTISTS!

What and who keep 1D humming along?

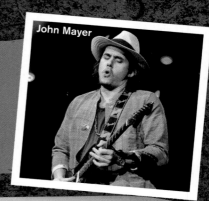

John Mayer

LIAM'S **TOP 5 SONGS THAT MAKE HIM SMILE**

1) "I Don't Trust Myself" by John Mayer
2) "I'm Yours" by Jason Mraz
3) "Thinking of Me" by Olly Murs
4) "Who Let the Dogs Out?" by the Baha Men
5) "Happy Birthday"—*"cause it makes everybody smile!"*

Lady Antebellum

HARRY'S **TOP 5 SONGS TO GET READY TO**

1) "The A Team" by Ed Sheeran
2) "Skinny Love" by Birdy
3) "Need You Now" by Lady Antebellum
4) "Showgirl" by Bluey Robinson
5) "What Makes you Beautiful" by One Direction (*"It's our single!"*)

LOUIS'S **TOP 5 FAVORITE ARTISTS**

1) The Fray
2) James Morrison
3) Pink (*"She's so amazing – I love her music!"*)
4) Adele (*"Her last album was fantastic!"*)
5) Katy Perry

Adele

Usher

ZAYN'S **TOP 5 ROMANTIC SONGS**

1)"Can U Help Me?" by Usher
2) "U Got It Bad" by Usher
3) "Superman" by Robin Thicke
4) "Can U Believe?" by Robin Thicke (*"Anything by him."*)
5) "So Sick" by Ne-Yo

NIALL'S **TOP 5 SONGS TO GET READY TO**

1) "I Gotta Feeling" by the Black Eyed Peas
2) "Party Rock Anthem" by LMFAO (*"So bouncy!"*)
3) "I'm Not Alone" by Calvin Harris (*"You can't beat it!"*)
4) "Dynamite" by Taio Cruz (*"That's a good one!"*)
5) "On the Floor" by Jennifer Lopez

LMFAO

1D'S SOCCER FAVES

In an interview with *The People*, the 1D guys stood up for their teams.

Harry: Manchester United—"I used to go a lot but it has become more difficult now because of the band... but I can't really complain—we're having the time of our lives."

Zayn: Manchester United, although—"I've never been to one of their games."

Louis: Manchester United—"I'm a lifelong fan."

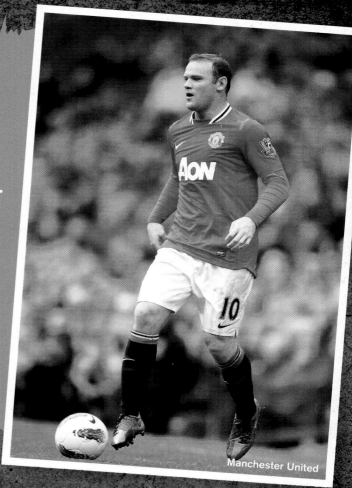

Manchester United

Derby County

Niall: Derby County—"My dad supports them though sometimes it's been a bit heartbreaking!"

West Bromwich Albion

Liam: West Bromwich Albion—"My dad is from West Brom and I wasn't allowed in my uncle's house unless I supported them, so I had no choice!"

(The People)

97

BRIT SPEAK
Learn How to Talk Like 1D

Every language has its unique expressions, its forms of lingo—kind of like each new generation has its own slang. Your grandmother might have written SWAK on the back of a love letter to her boyfriend—by which she meant "Sealed With A Kiss." Your mom might have referred to the cool boy at school as "bad"—which really meant she thought he was a hottie. And if someone was super upset, she might have said, "Take a chill pill!"

Of course, Facebook, Twitter, and other social media platforms make some slang universal, but other lingo is distinctive to a country or region. If you listen to 1D's Harry, Louis, Niall, Zayn, or Laim for more than a minute, you will hear certain expressions pop up that are pure British Isles. We've come up with a short dictionary to help fans on this side of the Atlantic help decipher what the boys are talking about. Read it, study it. There's a quiz coming up!

Banko: Bank holiday, as in, "New Year's Day is a banko."

Bird: Girlfriend, as in, "She's my bird."

Biscuit or Bikkie Cookie, as in, "Liam loves chocolate-chip bikkies."

Blimey: An expression of annoyance or surprise, as in, "Blimey, my car's got a ticket on it!"

Bloke: A guy, as in, "That bloke is a friend of Niall's."

Bloody: Very, as in, "*Up All Night* is bloody awesome!"

Bloomin': Very, as in, "It's bloomin' crowded it in here!"

Bugger Off: Go away, as in, "Stop annoying me, bugger off!"

Brilliant or Brill: Excellent, as in, "'What Makes You Beautiful' is a totally brilliant [or brill] song!"

Bum: Backside, as in, "Harry fell flat on his bum on stage!"

Chat Up: Flirt, as in, "I like that girl over there. I'm going to chat her up."

Cheeky: Brazen, as in, "Those 1D boys are really cheeky!"

Chips: French fries, as in, "I'm going for some fish and chips."

Crisps: Potato chips, as in, "I've got the munchies—pass those crisps."

Daft: Crazy, as in, "You think Harry should cut his hair—are you daft?"

Dodgy: Odd, suspect, as in, "I'm not sure of his motives—he seems dodgy."

Fancy: To be attracted to someone, as in, "Louis fancies Eleanor."

Fit: Physically attractive, as in, "That girl is fit!"

Flat: Apartment, as in, "Harry and Louis shared a luxury flat in London after *The X Factor*."

Footy: Football (British soccer), as in, "Harry's favorite footy team is Manchester United."

Get On: Have chemistry with, as in, "Louis, Harry, Liam, Niall, and Zayn really get on."

Gob: Mouth, as in, "He never shuts his gob!"

Jack-the-Lad: Carefree or brash young lad, as in, "Justin Bieber was Jack-the-Lad on the Taylor Swift *Punk'd* episode!"

Jam: Jelly fruit spread, as in, "Harry loves strawberry jam." [In England, Jelly is a gelatin dessert, what we usually call Jell-O.]

Jolly: Day trip, as in, "Let's go to the country for a jolly."

Jumper: Sweater, as in, "When he's a bit cold, Louis puts on his jumper."

Kip: A nap, as in, "Shhh, Liam is catching a kip right now."

Lad: Boy or young man, as in, "Love those 1D lads!"

Mad: Nutty, as in, "Those 1D fans waiting for hours on line are mad!"

Mates: Friends or buddies, as in, "Louis and Harry are best mates."

Mum: Mother, as in, "Johanna Tomlinson is Louis's mum."

Pants: Underpants, as in what should be under your trousers.

Posh: Fancy, chic, upscale, as in, "That girl seems a bit posh for our lad Harry."

Row: Argument, as in, "The 1D lads never get into rows—they discuss any problem they have."

Rubbish: Not good, not true, as in, "Those rumors about Zayn and Miranda Cosgrove are total rubbish!"

Sithee: Good-bye, as in, "The concert's over, sithee!"

Straight Away: Right now, as in, "We're getting those 1D tickets straight away."

Takeaway: Takeout food, as in, "When Niall doesn't have time to eat at Nando's, he does takeaway."

Trousers: Pants, as in, "Louis loves to wear suspenders with his trousers."

Wicked: Very cool, as in, "One Direction's concert at Radio City Music Hall was wicked!"

Washing: Laundry, as in, "Even when Harry wasn't living at home, he took his washing back for his mum to do."

Fill in the Blanks

1 If you wanted to compliment Louis' sweater, you would say, "I really like your _____."

2 If you were out on a date with Harry, you might go to the local restaurant and get _____, then go back home with it and watch a DVD."

3 You want to tell the 1D guys that *Up All Night* is the best album ever. You might say, "Your CD is totally _____!"

4 You are hungry for something crispy and salty. You might say, "I'm in the mood for some fish and _____."

5 Danielle Peazer is Liam's girlfriend. He might call her his "_____."

6 The boys of 1D love to watch "_____."

7 The woman who gave birth to Zayn Malik is his _____.

8 Those 1D guys are really good looking—they're, "_____."

9 1D's schedule is so hectic that the boys often catch a quick _____ on a plane.

10 The quiz is over! "_____."

ANSWERS: 1) Jumper; 2) Takeaway; 3) Brilliant or brill; 4) Chips; 5) Bird; 6) Footie as in football or soccer; 7) Mum; 8) Fit; 9) Kip; 10) Sithee

I.D. ON 1D: HARRY

How much do you know about 1D? Do you know Harry's most annoying habit? Do you know Niall's nickname in Ireland? Louis's biggest mistake? Zayn's biggest fear? Liam's little-known sports talents? Whether you're 1D trivia-challenged or you're on course to become the biggest 1D expert ever, dive into these factoids and really get to know 1D's fabulous five!

HARRY...QUICK FACTS

FULL NAME: Harry Edward Styles

BIRTHDAY: February 1, 1994

ASTRO SIGN: Aquarius

BIRTHPLACE: Evesham, England

CHILDHOOD RESIDENCE: Holmes Chapel, England

EYES/HAIR: green/brown

PARENTS: mother, Anne; father, Des (divorced); stepfather Robin

SIBLING: older sister, Gemma

SCHOOL: Holmes Chapel Comprehensive School

FIRST BAND: White Eskimo

FIRST JOB: bakery

EARLY MUSICAL INFLUENCES: Elvis Presley, The Beatles, Queen

CURRENT MUSICAL INFLUENCES: Chris Martin of Coldplay, Ed Sheeran

CURRENT FAVORITE MUSICAL ARTISTS: Foster the People, Coldplay, Kings of Leon

ONE DIRECTION PERSONA: The Flirt

ONE DIRECTION INSIDE JOKE: Harry and Louis are best buds and the two are sometimes called "Larry Stylinson"

MOST ANNOYING HABIT: He snores!

BIGGEST FEAR: roller-coasters

FUN TALENT: juggling

LITTLE KNOWN TALENT: speaks French fluently

LITTLE KNOWN TALENT 2: loves to cook

FAVORITE FOOD: tacos

FAVORITE DRINKS: water, apple juice

FAVORITE TV SHOW: *Friends*—Ross is his favorite character

FAVORITE ANIMALS: turtles

I.D. ON 1D: NIALL

NIALL...QUICK FACTS

FULL NAME: Niall James Horan

BIRTHDAY: November 13, 1993

ASTRO SIGN: Virgo

BIRTHPLACE: Mullingar, Republic of Ireland

EYES/HAIR: blue/blonde

PARENTS: mother, Maura; father, Bobby (divorced)

SIBLING: older brother, Greg

PET: cat, Jess

SCHOOL: Coláiste Mhuire

PRE-1D ALTERNATE CAREER GOAL: sound engineer

INSTRUMENT: guitar

FIRST CHILDHOOD MEMORY: singing

LOCAL NICKNAME: "The Irish Justin Bieber"

EARLY MUSICAL INFLUENCES: Frank Sinatra, Don Henley

CURRENT FAVORITE MUSICAL ARTISTS: Michael Bublé, Justin Bieber

ONE DIRECTION PERSONA: The Shopper

STRANGEST HABIT: talks in his sleep

FUN FACT: Katy Perry was on the 2010 *The X Factor* judging panel and voted Niall, as a solo act, to Boot Camp

LITTLE KNOWN FACT: Niall is ticklish— under his arms!

FAVORITE SPORT: football (soccer)

FAVORITE PASTIME: eating!

FAVORITE FOODS: Chinese, Japanese, Italian

FAVORITE CANDY: Galaxy chocolate

FAVORITE RESTAURANT: Nando's

FAVORITE SNACK: pistachio nuts

FAVORTIE ACTOR: Liam Neeson

FAVORITE TV SHOW: *Two and a Half Men*

FAVORITE MOVIE: Grease

FAVORITE AFTERSHAVE: Armani Mania

BOXERS OR BRIEFS: Calvin Klein boxers

HATES TO WEAR: cardigans

I.D. ON ID: LOUIS

LOUIS...QUICK FACTS

FULL NAME: Louis William Tomlinson

BIRTHDAY: December 24, 1991

ASTRO SIGN: Capricorn

BIRTHPLACE: Doncaster, England

EYES/HAIR: blue/light brown

PARENTS: mother, Johanna ("Jay"); father, Mark

SIBLINGS: younger sisters Charlotte, Félicité, and twins Daisy and Phoebe

FIRST PET: dog, Ted

SCHOOLS: Hall Cross School and the Hayfield School.

INSTRUMENT: piano

FIRST SCHOOL MUSICAL: Grease—he played Danny Zuko

FIRST NON-SHOW BIZ JOB: Toys R Us

FIRST SHOW BIZ JOB: small parts in British TV shows, *If I Had You* and *Waterloo Road*

CURRENT FAVORITE MUSICAL ARTISTS: The Fray, James Morrison, Ed Sheeran

ONE DIRECTION PERSONA: The Leader

WORST HABIT: biting his nails

BIGGEST FEAR: going bald!

BIGGEST ID MISTAKE: saying he likes girls who eat carrots—he's now showered with the veggie everywhere he goes. Ouch!

FUN FACT: never wears socks

FAVORITE ACTOR: Jim Carrey

FAVORITE SPORTS: football (soccer), tennis

FAVORITE FOOD: Pizza Hut's cookie dough dessert

FAVORITE DRINK: Yorkshire Tea

FAVORITE SANDWICH: prawn, mayo with prawn cocktail crisps on the side

FAVORITE SONG: The Fray's "Look After You"

FAVORITE MOVIE: Forrest Gump

FAVORITE AFTERSHAVE: Hollister

I.D. ON 1D: ZAYN

ZAYN...QUICK FACTS

FULL NAME: Zain Javadd "Zayn" Malik

BIRTHDAY: January 12, 1993

ASTRO SIGN: Capricorn

BIRTHPLACE: Bradford, England

CHILDHOOD RESIDENCE: East Bowling, England

EYES/HAIR: brown/black

PARENTS: mother, Tricia; father, Yaser

SIBLINGS: sisters, Doniya, Waliyha and Safaa

PETS: dog, Boris; two cats, Rolo and Tom

SCHOOL: Tong High School

CHILDHOOD COLLECTION: comic books

INSTRUMENT: guitar

PRE-1D ALTERNATE CAREER GOAL: English, drama or science teacher

FAVORITE BOY BAND: *NSYNC

FAVORITE MUSICAL GENRE: R&B and rap

FAVORITE CURRENT MUSICAL ARTIST: Bruno Mars

ONE DIRECTION PERSONA: The Gorgeous One

MOST HORRIBLE HABIT HE KICKED: smoking cigarettes—he doesn't anymore!

BIGGEST FEAR: water—he can't swim

LITTLE KNOWN FACT: Before 1D Zayn had never left England and didn't have a passport!

LITTLE KNOWN FACT 2: Zayn felt so uncomfortable dancing that when he first auditioned for *The X Factor*, he always got nervous before he had to take the stage.

FAVORITE BOOK SERIES: Harry Potter

FAVORITE HOBBY: drawing

FAVORITE ETHNIC FOOD: samosas, deep-fried Indian snacks

FAVORITE FOOD: chicken

FAVORITE SAYING: "Vas happenin'?"

FAVORITE MOVIE: Scarface

FAVORITE SONG: Michael Jackson's "Thriller"

FAVORITE GROOMING PRODUCT: hair wax

FUN FACT: He has seven tattoos—a Yin Yang on his wrist; a picture of crossed fingers on his forearm; his granddad's name, Walter, in Arabic on his chest; a "born lucky" symbol; a playing card on his stomach and an inscription in Arabic across his collarbone that means "be true to who you are," and a heart on his stomach.

I.D. ON ID: LIAM

LIAM...QUICK FACTS

FULL NAME: Liam James Payne

BIRTHDAY: August 29, 1993

ASTRO SIGN: Virgo

BIRTHPLACE: Wolverhampton, England

EYES/HAIR: brown/light brown

PARENTS: mother, Karen; father, Geoff

SIBLINGS: older sisters, Ruth and Nicola

SCHOOL: City of Wolverhampton College

INSTRUMENTS: guitar and piano

EARLY MUSICAL INFLUENCES: Take That's Gary Barlow, Justin Timberlake

ONE DIRECTION PERSONA: The Responsible One

WORST HABIT: worrying

BIGGEST FEAR: spoons—he uses them at home, but not in restaurants

LITTLE KNOWN TALENT: sprinting—he was on the reserve list for the 2012 Summer Olympics

LITTLE KNOWN TALENT 2: boxing—he began studying it after being bullied in school

LITTLE KNOWN TALENT 3: beatbox

FAVORITE SONG: "Happy Birthday"—and he also loves presents!

FAVORITE ACTORS: Will Smith, Johnny Depp, Orlando Bloom

FAVORITE SPORT: basketball

FAVORITE FOOD: ham sandwiches

FAVORITE SNACK: chocolate

FAVORITE TOY: Legos

FAVORITE MOVIES: the *Toy Story* films

FAVORITE COUNTRY: the United States

SIGNATURE POSE: thumbs up!

MEET AND GREET

When 1D hit the road in America, their loyal Directioneers couldn't have been more supportive. At each and every appearance fans camped out for hours just to catch a glimpse of Harry, Niall, Liam, Louis, and Zayn. Here are just a few stops along the way.

February 24, 2012: (left to right) Zayn, Louis, Harry, Niall, and Liam make a morning visit to Chicago's 103.5 KISS FM radio station. They were totally gaga over the news they got three days earlier—*Up All Night* debuted at No. 1 on the *Billboard 200* album chart. Niall, who was in a taxicab when he found out, told reporters, "I freaked out!" And then he called all his friends!

March 11, 2012: (left to right) Harry, Louis, Liam, Zayn, and Niall say hello at the Westfield Sunrise Mall in Massapequa, NY. Fans were there bright and early so they could be among the first 1,000 Directioneers to show up. Those lucky fans got to rush the guys for autographs.

Harry, Louis, Liam, Zayn, and Niall signed Up All Night CDs for fans at New York City's J&R music store.

March 17, 2012: (left to right) Louis, Zayn, and Liam (Niall and Harry are out of shot) take fan questions on their visit to Bala Cynwyd, PA's Q102 iHeartRadio, where they announced their 2012 summer tour dates. But they weren't the only stars of the event—a local animal shelter brought some puppies for the guys to cuddle while they sang "What Makes You Beautiful." Niall and Zayn bonded immediately with the canine cuties, but Harry got a downright cheeky pooch who didn't want to be held! Guess the pup wasn't a Directioneer!

March 17, 2012: (left to right) Louis, Harry, Liam, Zayn, and Niall made another stop on March 17, St. Patrick's Day. Irish-born Niall was all Erin Go Bragh that day at the group's Walmart appearance in Somerdale, NJ. Niall shows off the Irish flag and Harry gives him a thumbs-up.

FANTASIA

Can you find 1D?
(Answer below)

"One of our fans made us all dog tags with our names on them—that was pretty amazing."
—Harry (Virgin Music Red Room)

Hysteria! Madness! Flash mobs! That's how the press have described fan reaction to 1D. When Directioneers show up to support one of the most popular bands in the world today the scene can get crazy. But it's all good, because what brings all these girls together is adoration. They absolutely love One Direction, and Niall, Harry, Zayn, Louis, and Liam love them right back. The guys credit their success to the fans they had way back during *The X Factor*, and to the ones that have joined the club since then. They enjoy the chance to actually meet their fans. And it makes them happy to look out in an audience and see banners and flags and T-shirts emblazoned with their names. No wonder they seem to be smiling all the time!

"I can't believe that they're real! They're so beautiful! I even got to take a picture with Paul!" (Paul is Paul Higgins, 1D's bodyguard and tour manager.)
—A fan at 1D's *Today* appearance in March 2012 (*Entertainment Weekly*)

"Yesterday we were doing a meet-and-greet where we meet fans just before we go on stage at the concert. This girl asked to lick my face! That was really random!"
—Liam (*scholastic.com*)

"Since we've been here, we did Radio City [Music Hall in New York City] with Big Time Rush and when we were leaving the venue, there were a lot of people waiting outside for us and it was like the movies. We were trying to drive away. [Fans] were running through traffic. It was literally something you'd see in a movie."
—Niall (*MTV News*)

TEST YOUR 1D IQ
Word Scramble

1D Brainiacs, put your thinking caps on! We scrambled up the letters of the following phrases, so it's up to you to put them in the correct order and spell out the words that have a special 1D meaning. Good luck!

1 PU LAL GTINH
1D's debut album

2 GBI EMIT SHUR
1D opened for this band on its first U.S. tour

3 HET EUNALM ZITRO HOWS
The name of the *Saturday Night Live* skit 1D starred in

4 ERESINOTECRID
The nickname of 1D fans

5 MOINS LEWLOC
1D's musical mentor

6 RANDAMI VORGSEOC
The star of the Nick show *iCarly*

7 GOI ENO TCIEORNDI
The name of the *iCarly* episode 1D starred in

8 LYNAM ECHBA
The Sydney, Australia, beach where Louis and Liam went surfing

9 TKA HET AOLKA
The name of the animal 1D embraced in Australia

10 HAYWLAI, YDNOIA, & AAASF
Zayn's sisters

11 VERTNOWOLMHPA
Liam's hometown

12 YKAT RREPY
One of Louis's celebrity crushes

13 DDIVA MBAEHCK
Niall's favorite soccer player

14 RMEATNSCEH DUENTI
Zayn's favorite soccer team

15 ESIEHT
British slang for good-bye

16 LVISE YEPRLSE
Harry's rock & roll idol

17 HET X CFAROT
The TV show that gave 1D their start

IDENTIFY THE 1D QUOTE

Outta the mouths of babes! Do you recognize these quotes from the previous pages of this book? If you are really 1D Directioneers, you should be able to match Niall, Harry, Liam, Louis, or Zayn with the following pearls!

1 "I always tell [the guys] jokes, then everyone goes silent. They all shake their heads and say to me, 'That wasn't funny.'" (*Bop*)

2 "I was always a big Frank Sinatra fan from a very young age; I don't know where I caught that. I might have just heard it on the radio. Maybe my family had some CDs, but I was always a singer and a mover." (*Life Story*)

3 "We thought it could be the same few hundred people Tweeting us over and over again [from America] . . . Until we got to America we didn't realize how crazy it was." (*The Sun*)

4 "I was about 12 or 13 when I started taking pride in my appearance. I even used to get up half an hour earlier than my sister so I could do my hair. (*The Sun*)

5 "I like someone who can take a bit of banter, have a laugh, and who likes the same things as me—if you go out with me, you have to want to come to a football match . . . I like the natural look!" (*Dare To Dream: Life As One Direction*)

6 "I went to dinner with a girl, and she just didn't speak! I started asking quite elaborate questions and I'm pretty sure she found some way to answer with a yes or no. It made me really tired. By the end of the night I was like, 'Thank God that's over!'" (*M* magazine)

7 "I came to America quite a bit as a kid. Applebee's is the best restaurant!" (*Twist*)

8 "I am a big Michael Jackson fan. He was a real inspiration and had so many great songs. . . . I'd like to adopt a chimpanzee and build an eternal friendship. That would be amazing." (On Air With Ryan Seacrest)

9 "[During the past year] I've learnt how much you can fit into a suitcase. I mean literally you can fit so much in. You think it won't shut, but you get a couple of people to sit on it and job done." (*First News*)

10 "It's been amazing being over here in the States. We couldn't believe the amount of people that showed up to the *Today* show. . . . We couldn't have asked for any more and we never really imagined any of this!" (On Air With Ryan Seacrest)

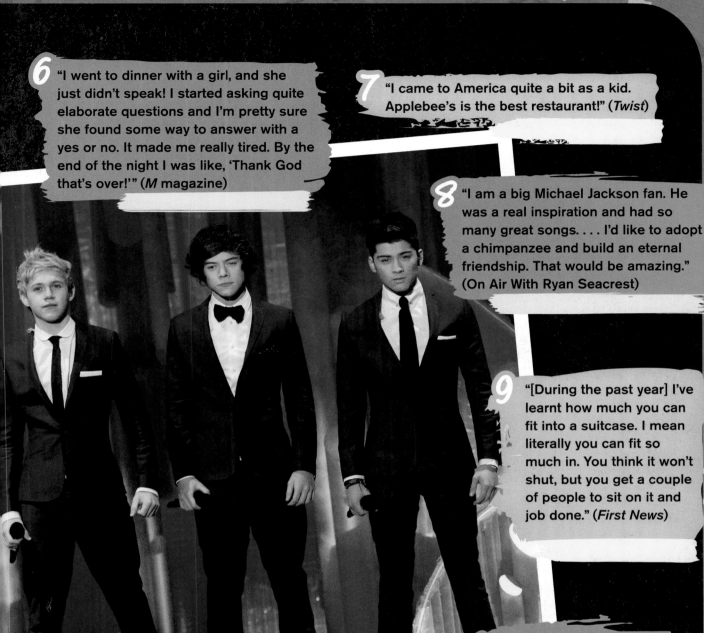

ANSWERS: 1) Harry; 2) Niall; 3) Zayn; 4) Zayn; 5) Niall; 6) Harry; 7) Liam; 8) Liam; 9) Louis; 10) Liam

1D TRUE OR FALSE QUIZ

Here's another brainteaser to test your 1D IQ. It's easy—just answer the questions as True or False. All the backup info you need is in the pages of this book. Have fun!

1 The first single release from 1D's *Up All Night* was "What Makes You Beautiful" in the U.S., but "One Thing" in England.
True or False?

2 1D drew thousands of fans to New York City's Central Park for their *Today* show concert in March 2012.
True or False?

3 One Direction's *iCarly* episode was originally named "iGot Jungle Worms," and then changed to "iGo One Direction."
True or False?

4 When 1D met First Lady Michelle Obama at the 2012 Nickelodeon Kids' Choice Awards, she invited them to come to the White House for the annual Easter Egg Roll.
True or False?

5 Harry once shaved his head and put slits in his eyebrows to appear a little bit "gangsta."
True or False?

6 Louis belonged to a band named The Rogue when he was still in school.
True or False?

7 1D opened for the Jonas Brothers at Radio City Music Hall in March 2012.
True or False?

8 Niall once dreamed about being a soccer player.
True or False?

9 Applebee's is Liam's favorite restaurant in America.
True or False?

10 Harry's favorite character on the TV show *Friends* is "Chandler."
True or False?

11 Niall has a younger brother named Greg.
True or False?

12 When Zayn was younger he collected model airplanes.
True or False?

13 Harry got a cake in the face during a visit to Z-100's Elvis Duran and the Morning Show in N.Y.C.
True or False?

14 Zayn has a phobia about spoons.
True or False?

15 Louis's younger twin sisters are named Daisy and Phoebe.
True or False?

16 Liam's all-time favorite song is Michael Jackson's "Thriller."
True or False?

17 Niall has been called the "Irish Justin Bieber."
True or False?

18 Harry says his most annoying habit is biting his nails.
True or False?

19 Harry, Louis, and Zayn are all big fans of the British soccer team Manchester United.
True or False?

20 One of Zayn's favorite romantic songs is "Can You Help Me?" by Usher.
True or False?

ANSWERS: 1) False—it was "What Makes You Beautiful" in both the U.S. and England; 2) False—the concert was held at Rockefeller Center Plaza; 3) True; 4) True; 5) False—it was Zayn; 6) True; 7) False—1D opened for Big Time Rush.; 8) True; 9) True; 10) False—it's Ross; 11) False—Greg is Niall's older brother; 12) False—he collected comic books; 13) True; 14) False—it's Liam who's afraid of using spoons; 15) True; 16) True; 17) True; 18) False—most annoying habit is snoring; 19) True; 20) True

CAUGHT ON CAMERA!

Silly? Yes. Goofy? Sometimes. Perhaps a *bit* naughty? Occasionally. But always fun! The boys of 1D behave like a barrel full of monkeys and a pile of puppies all rolled into one. We leave you with a gallery of pics documenting just a few choice moments....

PHOTO CREDITS

Front Cover: Michael Kovac/WireImage/Getty Images (group), Venturelli/Getty Images (performing). 3: Dave Hogan/Getty Images. 7: Newspix/Rex/Rex USA. 8–9: Beretta/Sims/Rex/Rex USA. 11–13: Dave Hogan/Getty Images (all). 14: Eamonn McCormack/WireImage/Getty Images. 15: David Fisher/Rex/Rex USA. 16: George Pimentel/WireImage/Getty Images. 17: NBC/NBCUniversal/Getty Images. 19: IBL/Rex/Rex USA. 21: Matt Baron/ BEImages (all). 22–23: Danny Martindale/Getty Images. 25: IBL/Rex/Rex USA. 26: Zerna/Newspix/Rex/Rex USA. 27: Matt Baron/BEImages (all). 28–29: Jon Furniss/WireImage/Getty Images. 30–32: © Splash News/Corbis (all). 33: © Splash News/Corbis (fans, LAX), Matt Baron/BEImages (backstage). 34: Larry Busacca/Getty Images. 35: Matt Baron/BEImages (all). 36: Erik Pendzich/Rex USA (fans), Picture Perfect/Rex USA (performing). 37: Picture Perfect/Rex USA (all). 38: Everett Collection/Rex USA (Harry), Picture Perfect/Rex USA (Liam, Zayn). 39: Erik Pendzich/Rex USA (Louis), Matt Baron/BEImages (Niall). 40: © Splash News/Corbis (all). 41: Adam Bettcher/ Getty Images (all). 42: Christopher Polk/Getty Images (red carpet), Kevork Djansezian/Getty Images (live show). 43: © Splash News/Corbis. 44–46: Newspix/Rex/Rex USA (all). 47: Newspix/Rex/Rex USA (radio), Nikki To/Rex/ Rex USA (fans). 48: © Splash News/Corbis. 49–51: Newspix/Rex/Rex USA (all). 52: © Splash News/Corbis. 53: Newspix/Rex/Rex USA (all). 54–55: Hunter/Newspix/Rex/Rex USA (all). 56–57: Newspix/Nathan Richter/Rex/Rex USA (all). 58–59: Scott Barbour/Getty Images (all). 60–61: © Splash News/Corbis (all). 63: IBL/Rex/Rex USA.

65: Matt Baron/BEImages (all). 66–67: Owen Sweeney/Rex/Rex USA. 69: IBL/Rex/Rex USA. 71: Matt Baron/ BEImages (all). 72–73: Newspix/Rex/Rex USA. 75: IBL/Rex/Rex USA. 77: Matt Baron/BEImages (all). 78–79: IBL/ Rex/Rex USA. 80–81: AGF s.r.l./Rex/Rex USA. 82¬–83: Nikki To/Rex/Rex USA (all). 84–85: NBC/NBCUniversal/ Getty Images (all). 86–87: Ken McKay/Rex/Rex USA (all). 88–89: Michael Kovac/WireImage/Getty Images (all). 90: Jonathan Hordle/Rex/Rex USA (Rosie), George Pimentel/WireImage/Getty Images (Zayn, Louis), Michael Buckner/ Getty Images (Natalie). 91: Jonathan Hordle/Rex/Rex USA (Leona), George Pimentel/WireImage/Getty Images (Liam, Harry, Niall), Picture Perfect/Rex USA (Kate), Hugh Thompson/Rex/Rex USA (Demi). 92–93: Matt Baron/ BEImages (all). 94: khunaspix/Shutterstock.com (astronaut), RTimages/Shutterstock.com (soccer player), T-Design/ Shutterstock.com (fireman), PRNewsFoto/Nickelodeon, SABAN (Ranger), Wojciech Beczynski/Shutterstock.com (SWAT). 95: trappy76/Shutterstock.com (Liberty), JustASC/Shutterstock.com (Hollywood), Alice/Shutterstock. com (Flag). 96: Lester Cohen/WireImage/Getty Images (John), Matt Baron/BEImages (Lady Antebellum), Richard Young/Rex/Rex USA (Adele), David Rowland/Rex/Rex USA (Usher), Richardson/Newspix/Rex/Rex USA (LMFAO). 97: Alex Livesey/Getty Images (Manchester), Ben Hoskins/Getty Images (Derby), Clint Hughes/Getty Images (Bromwich). 98: Geordie/Shutterstock.com. 99: Hannes Eichinger/Shutterstock.com (chips), AndreaAstes/Photos. com (crisps), Newspix/Rex/Rex USA (Harry), DSPA/Shutterstock.com (Manchester United), effe45/Shutterstock. com (jam), Nikki To/Rex/Rex USA (fan). 100: Raymond Mclean/Shutterstock.com (pants), Jim Smeal/BEImages (Miranda Cosgrove), McPix Ltd/Rex/Rex USA (Harry and Louis), Matt Baron/BEImages (Louis). 103–111: George Pimentel/WireImage/Getty Images (all). 112: Raymond Boyd/Michael Ochs Archives/Getty Images. 113: Janette Pellegrini/WireImage/Getty Images (holding up album, fans), Ilya S. Savenok/Getty Images (J&R). 114: Bill McCay/ WireImage/Getty Images (Zayn), MediaPunch Inc/Rex USA (Harry, radio). 115: Owen Sweeney/Rex/Rex USA (group, Niall), MediaPunch Inc/Rex USA (Harry). 116: IBL/Rex/Rex USA (airport, answer), Newspix/Rex/Rex USA (fans). 117: Newspix/Rex/Rex USA (sign, crowd, running, wedding dress), Beretta/Sims/Rex/Rex USA (Niall). 118: Jim Smeal/BEImages (Big Time Rush), McPix Ltd/Rex/Rex USA (Simon Cowell), NBC/NBCUniversal/Getty Images (SNL), Matt Baron/BEImages (Fans). 119: Offside/Rex/Rex USA (Manchester United), Jim Smeal/BEImages (Katy Perry, Miranda Cosgrove), Newspix/Nathan Richter/Rex/Rex USA (Zayn). 120–121: Ken McKay/Rex/Rex USA. 122: © Splash News/Corbis (iCarly), Kevork Djansezian/Getty Images (Obama), Rob Kim/Getty Images (Jonas). 123: rimira/Shutterstock.com (plane), Paul Zimmerman/WireImage/Getty Images (Harry), BuzzFoto/BuzzFoto/Getty Images (Justin), Rex USA (Thriller), Jim Smeal/BEImages (Usher). 124: Steve Meddle/Rex/Rex USA. 125: Everett Collection/Rex USA (Niall), Martin Karius/Rex/Rex USA (take a picture), Jon Furniss/WireImage/Getty Images (wrapping), Matt Baron/BEImages (Liam and Harry). 126: Bill McCay/Getty Images (Niall), Newspix/Rex/Rex USA (Liam, Harry), MediaPunch Inc/Rex USA (Silly String). 127: Newspix/Nathan Richter/Rex/Rex USA.